Rachel's Guide to FRUGAL LIVING & CAMPING

How to Survive and Thrive While Living Out of Your Car

Save Money & Experience True Freedom!

By

Rachel Clark

Copyrighted Material

Copyright © Savona Carrara Publishing House, 2022

All Rights Reserved.

Without limiting the rights under the copyright laws, no part of this publication may be reproduced, stored in or introduced into a retrieval system, or transmitted, in any form or by any means (electronic, mechanical, photocopying, recording or otherwise), without the prior written consent of the publisher of this book.

Savona Carrara Publishing House publishes its books and guides in a variety of electronic and print formats, Some content that appears in print may not be available in electronic format, and vice versa.

Cover Art Design

By

Jessica Thomson

First Edition

Contents

Chapter 1: What is Car Camping? 9

Pros and Cons of Car Camping..**12**

    Comfort 14

    Camping is Perfect 15

    Easy Intro 17

    It's Relaxing 18

    Cons to Consider 20

Emotional Preparation..**22**

    Prepare For the Worst 22

    Take Baby Steps 23

    Keep an Eye on the Weather 23

    Consider Your Comfort Level 23

    Prepare to Disconnect...26

    Food Changes 28

Types of Vehicles That are Best for Car Camping...................**28**

Chapter 2: Defining Stealth (Urban) Camping and Legalities.....38

Urban Camping..**44**

    Walmart parking lots...46

    Other big-box store parking lots 46

    Visitor centers 48

    Truck stops and rest areas 48

- Hotel and motel parking lots 49
- Trailheads 49
- Casino parking lots 49
- Small towns and gas stations 49

State Laws on Urban Camping 51

Chapter 3: How to Plan Your Trip: Gearing Up 58

Navigation 60
- Map 60
- Compass 60
- GPS Device 61
- Altimeter Watch 61

Survival Gear 62
- Headlamp and Extra Batteries 62
- Sun Protection 62
- First Aid 62
- Knife and Repair Kit 62
- Fire 63

Life Essentials 63
- Shelter 63
- Extra Food 64
- Extra Water 64
- Extra Clothes 64

Optional Gear 65

Sleeping Pad or a Mattress Pad 65

Tent 66

Sleeping Bags 66

Pillows and Blankets.. 66

Lamps 67

Camp Chairs and Foldable Tables 67

Kitchen Gear.. 68

Saving Storage Space 69

Separate things by size and use. 70

Get a cargo carrier. 71

Consider a cargo hammock. 72

Use the side door storage and get "behind the seat" organizers... 72

Get cargo bins. 72

Chapter 4: Car Camping With Kids 74

Make Lists 76

Plan Ahead 76

Bigger is Better 77

Camp Nearby 77

Buddy System 78

Chore Time 78

Be Organized 79

Play Time 79

Chapter 5: Finding Your Campsite 81

Campgrounds - Free to $50 Per Night 82

Federal Land Campgrounds 83

State Park Campgrounds 85

County Park Campgrounds 85

RV Parks - $35 to $50 Per Night 86

RV Resorts - $50 and Above 87

Chapter 6: On Meals and Menus: Simple Recipes 88

Cooking in the Wild 89

Plan your meals ahead of time 90

Prep your ingredients the day before. 90

Pack small 91

Reduce your cooking steps. 91

Learn to love your propane stove. 91

Breakfast Recipes 92

Easy Scrambled Eggs 92

Spam and Egg Sandwich 93

Campfire Hash 94

Lunch Recipes 95

Quick Soup Pasta 95

Buttered Chicken Steak 96

Cheesy Steak in a Wrap 97

Vegetables in Foil 97

Dinner Recipes 98

Beef in a Foil 98

Quick Pork and Mushroom Sauté 99

A Word On Campfires and Bears 100

Building a Fire 101

Dealing with Bears 105

Chapter 7: Survival 101 111

Water 111

Shelter 113

Food 113

Getting Help/Getting Lost 114

Keep Healthy 115

Chapter 8: Making A Living While Camping 116

Utility Considerations 117

Internet Connection 117

Mail and Deliveries 118

Electricity and Power 119

Change Your Tires 119

Modifications 120

Chapter 9: Camp Etiquette and Safety 122

    Etiquette..122

    Safety 126

    Emergency Preparedness 129

Conclusion 132

Chapter 1: What is Car Camping?

It's amazing to see the internet - or people in general, for that matter - change its perception of something so easily and so suddenly.

You see, back in the '90s - a year or so after acquiring a degree which I was just slowly realizing was something I'll never love or use - I moved to the city to start fresh. It was one of those years in your life that you face head-on with a smile on your face, thinking, "This is it - I'm a Big City girl now!" You find yourself picturing the days of your life playing out like one of those CW teen series, with the sassy clothes, the constant hair-flipping, and all the endless drama.

Of course, no matter how many of your days start off with a piece of croissant and a delicious cup of morning coffee, nothing will play out like how you want or dream it to be.

One thing leads to another, and your landlord is one paycheck away from kicking you out because you chose to rent a room in a Victorian townhome (with bare red brick walls) you definitely can't afford with your starting salary.

After a year of trying to hold it together and living in denial, I realized that balancing two part-time gigs on top of my high-stress full-time job was simply not working. I was not sleeping nor eating well, I was pouring everything into my rent and utilities, and it wasn't until after I blacked out on the front porch that I finally realized I needed to make drastic changes in my life.

The hardest thing for me to do was to give up my quaint little piece of the city. Growing up, I always dreamed of having a small space just like that, just for me. But I know that in order to achieve my other long-term goals, I had to give up on that dream and move out. Once I let go of my flat, I discovered it was easier to downsize.

In the end, I made the decision to move into my car. A friend from home recommended that I try it for myself and advised that I ease into it. So, I started going on road trips by myself, where I essentially began camping in my car, sometimes a few weekends at a time, then gradually to weeks.

Needless to say, I was forced to live life in a minimalist manner. In the end, living in my car turned out to be a good reset button for me. I was able to look at my life from a different perspective and was able to understand what I actually needed and wanted.

But for the uninitiated, you might balk at the thought of squeezing into your car's back seats for a good night's sleep. Although it may sound like it, car camping doesn't mean you have to sleep in your car. The most general definition you can find on the internet is "to camp anywhere you can drive to and park your car." So once you reach your destination, you can either choose to sleep in your car - if it's big enough - or bring with you a tent where you can sleep.

But why car camping instead of bringing along a 30-feet long RV where everything can fit?

I rented and lived in an RV for a while, around a year after I decided to live in my car. Since I stayed in the city most of the time because of my job, I found that the RV is a mess to drive around with. Sure, the insides can be more spacious - class A motorhomes reach 40 feet in length. But can you imagine turning a corner with that cumbersome thing without stopping both sides of traffic in a two-lane street? I gave up on the RV after a week and moved to an SUV.

Obviously, something smaller than a 30-foot RV is going to be a lot easier to drive and bring around - not to mention you can do away with the special license and the plethora of various road restrictions that come with driving a huge monster of a vehicle.

Pros and Cons of Car Camping

I have tried backpacking in my university days through the heady warm tropics of Asia. It is definitely a rewarding experience, I can tell you that. I have met so many friends. I stayed the night in some beautiful bed and breakfasts and in shady traveler dormitories. I lugged that heavy backpack with me everywhere, and climbed and trekked through the mountains and jungles, and woke up in my one-person tent among a sea of clouds shivering in the cold.

But sadly, as I grew older, I am ashamed to say that I might have lost my sense of adventure. When I was younger, I could live through everything and sleep everywhere, but things, priorities, and your body do change as you grow older. I gave myself 1 year of freedom before jumping back to the world of academics. Then I went with the flow of humanity, finally moved out of my parents' house, got a job, and found my way of living my dream in the big city.

But my circumstances changing did have a silver lining. I guess when I was living in my cozy little apartment, I wanted to lose myself in the comfort of things, in the everyday mundaneness of life and material needs. However, deciding to live in my car brought back a small slice of that sense of adventure. It was like a camping trip for me every weekend.

When I was finally earning enough, I chose to live somewhere outside the city for a while. Far enough to feel the calm of nature but near enough to the city, so my job is just an hour away. The commute time for me is a sensible trade-off to my weekend camping trips. I rented then bought an SUV and started to hoard an extensive array of camping goods.

I loved car camping so much that when it's raining, I sometimes take the car and pitch a tent on one of those picnic areas near where I live. I stay inside my tent and fall asleep to the sound of the rain gently pattering against the tent walls.

Comfort

You don't have to worry about being uncomfortable.

As opposed to backpacking, where you need to be absolutely economical about space and weight, in car camping, you can bring almost anything you like with you (provided it can fit inside your car). And since you would be pitching your tent right next to your car, that Dutch oven you want to bring with you to cook your grandmother's infamous beef stew to the sound of waves lapping against the shorelines of a peaceful lake won't be left all alone in your house.

Speaking of gear, with the influx of new car camping and camping enthusiasts, companies have been more than happy to provide a wide array of goods for you to throw your money on. You can have your pick of different kinds of tents, chairs, foldable cookers, and benches. The choices will make you dizzy. And frankly, watching ASMR car camping YouTubers using the latest gadgets just makes me want to go order everything online. Personally, I have been recently tempted to buy a new tent. It was a battle between a glamorous bell tent and a minimalist rooftop tent.

And if you are worried about electricity and fresh water, you'll be happy to know that there's no shortage of well-equipped campsites which can provide sites with plenty of hookups so you can stay for days or weeks on end if you find yourself suddenly enjoying the car camping life too much.

Camping is Perfect

Camping is the perfect form of travel during these times.

The situation of the world right now just feels weird. It's like everything is off-kilter, and I definitely feel like we've just slipped into a parallel universe and are now living in a post-apocalyptic/dystopian era where Liam Neeson is the only Chosen One who can save the world.

As embarrassing as it is to say, I have grown to be increasingly cautious as I grow older - so when I finally emerged from my apartment, the only form of travel I was comfortable with was my beloved car camping trips.

I am outside; I feel the wind in my hair and the cold smoothness of stones in the river under my feet. And at the same time, I am in less danger of catching whatever is floating or is being expelled from the respiratory tracts of my fellow humans.

And if you are still having doubts about the safety of it all, maybe an article from Forbes can ease your worries. They declared that camping is the best form of travel a human can do during the pandemic. It is the ultimate socially distant form of travel as you are going to be amongst nature.

Easy Intro

Car camping is the perfect way to experience camping if you are a beginner.

Camping, I think, is addictive. While most human beings have common misconceptions about the lack of cellular connection sites and the overabundance of mosquitoes, what a lot of people don't know is that camping is actually pretty comfortable and easy. You do not have to make your own tents from twigs and branches, and no, you absolutely do not need to cut off your own arm or eat insects to survive.

Car camping sits in the Goldilocks zone of the camping world. You can bring as many types of luxuries as you want to make your trip comfortable, but you will be limited by the size of your chosen vehicle's trunk space. Granted, you can bring a lot more with you when you camp with an RV, but the bigger size of the vehicle also brings with it more responsibilities that a beginner like you might not be prepared for.

The car also offers more mobility - that's why large families camping in a big RV would usually have a towable vehicle dragging along behind their Class A motorhomes. They can leave the RV in a campsite and use the car to reach areas where an RV would not be able to fit.

And when you start car camping, you will find that the car being right next to your camp is very forgiving. For beginners, it is not unusual to forget to pack an essential here and there, but when you're car camping, a quick trip out of the campsite for a supply run is as easy as 1, 2, 3.

This is why for beginners, I would recommend you ease into the camping world by doing car camping first. And if you like it well enough, you can then proceed to either go bigger by buying or renting an RV or go more basic by going backpacking. In the end, it really depends on your level of comfort.

It's Relaxing

Relaxing is another word for car camping.

If you have a bad back like me, you'll be happy to know that you won't have to strain your back for hours on end carrying your tools and food with you like you would when you go backpacking. Because of this, car camping is relatively stress-free, with zero physical exertion on your part.

If you think having an RV is the epitome of comfort when camping, I urge you to think again. RVs are basically houses on wheels, no matter how big or small an RV is. With an RV, you would need to think about a lot of things, like emptying out the black and grey tanks (gross), cleaning them (double gross), what types of chemicals to use, and where to properly AND ENVIRONMENTALLY (this is so important) dump the smelly contents of your black tank.

Other than that, you would need to worry about the pipes, the antifreeze, the hookups, the alarms, the generators, and countless other things. What's the difference between a back-in and a pull-through site? You can throw that out the window because, with car camping, you won't need to worry about any of those.

But for the record, a pull-through site means that the campsite has a separate entrance and exit, so when you park your giant of a motorhome, you would not need to trouble yourself with backing out and doing a 16 point U-turn in order to leave your site. You can just "pull through" out of your space and out into the exit. A back-in site is, as you guessed it, a site that has only one entrance and exit point, and you will need to be a master RV driver in order to properly pull out of your site and out of the camp.

A car, on the other hand, is like having a smaller RV in terms of storage. You have a lot more room in your car for storage and also, having the car beside your tent also means there's less setting up and cleaning up after. For example, a lot of people who choose to sleep in the car would have a simple setup at the back of the car with the back door raised up. With the back seats folded down flat, you can easily set up a comfy sleeping area for you and your loved one with just an inflatable mattress or sleeping bags. The door can provide shade, and a few well-placed small tables and camping chairs can provide the perfect setup for a picnic.

Cons to Consider

Of course, car camping, like all things in life, also has its cons.

You might have heard the saying that the hardest places to go to are usually the most rewarding. That is true most of the time. It would be harder to look for sites that would be accessible by car that can give you views of an endless sea of clouds with the sun just rising over the horizon. But there are magnificent sites that are accessible by car - it's just fewer, and you would absolutely need to do your research. If you want breathtaking views, it's not hard.

Most of the time, if you are just new to camping, you will stick to the regulated campsites. It would be easier, as you'll have everything you'll need. But the views might be the back of your neighbor's RV peeping through the trees. To experience better views, you'll need to go boondocking.

And if you're looking for more adventure, backpacking would probably be better for you. Car camping is adventurous, yes, especially if you are a city dweller who has only been out camping a handful of times in your life. But it will not give you the thrill of adventure that backpacking can. Keep in mind that your car will also go through dirt roads, and cleaning it is a pain.

Emotional Preparation

Even though I said that car camping is perfect for

beginners, it may still be a daunting undertaking for some concrete jungle dwellers. In car camping, your backseat or the tent is waiting for you on the other end of the ride, which you will eventually need to set up. Even though car camping is indeed less stressful than other forms of camping, you will need to put in some effort and preparation in the end.

Basically, what I'm saying is you will need to be prepared before you do go car camping, or any other form of camping, for that matter. It may sound slightly pessimistic, but it would be better if you prepare in advance for the worst case scenario every time - because camping, like life in general, won't always go as planned.

Prepare For the Worst

Always have back-ups for your back-up plans. Do not stop at Plan B - if needed, go through the whole alphabet. That may look and sound a bit excessive, but do whatever floats your boat and keeps that anxiety in check.

Take Baby Steps

Do ease yourself slowly into this new way of exploration. Start slow and near - take your car and go for day camping trips near the city and go on picnics first. You can then gradually decide to move further and further away from your home on your next travels. Afterward, try staying overnight in some nearby farms or campsites to get a feel for it.

Keep an Eye on the Weather

Also, keep in mind that the weather will not always be like what you want it to be during your trips. Sudden rainstorms, especially during the end of summer months, are not uncommon. That car camping trip you have planned by the river might not be a good idea if there are chances of rain - the river might swell, and the rushing waters might sweep you away.

Consider Your Comfort Level

Another thing that might be harder to prepare for is the lack of the amenities you would usually take for granted in the city, like the electricity, fresh water, concrete walls, and the all-important bathroom.

There are ways on how one person can relieve themselves when they're out with nature. When we are not parked in a well-equipped campsite with full amenities like hookups and bathhouses, we have to do our number 1s and 2s out in the wild. When I go take a dump, I grab my trusty trowel and head for the woods, dig a deep enough hole and proceed to do my business. I know it's shocking, but I actually prefer it to emptying out a black tank. No more lengthy procedures and careful handling of bio-hazardous waste - all I need to do is to dig, poop, and cover.

Come to terms with doing your excretory business out in the wild first before considering car camping off the grid. If you are uncomfortable with the idea, you can always choose to camp in campsites.

And while we are on the subject of hygiene, if you plan to car camp for day trips or just for the weekend, I'd wager you wouldn't be that concerned about showers.

It's not uncommon for long-time car campers who go boondocking - another term for going off the beaten path and communing with nature while a million miles from other humans and civilization - to forego baths altogether if it's just for a few days. Granted, it will make your car stink, especially if you plan to do other activities other than just lounging about. But if you are alone, it won't be that bad - I have a feeling you'll be immune to your own smell anyway. Just bring a lot of wet wipes.

Otherwise, like the above, choose campsites with bathhouses and a supply of fresh water - or better yet, choose a location that has a body of water! Take a dip in the lake or river to clean that grime off.

Another thing to consider is your choice of shelter and again your comfort level. There are tons of tents out there for you to choose from, from simple one-man bivy tents that can only accommodate 1 sleeping bag to nicer multi-room tents that are reminiscent of the tents the Weasleys had in the Quidditch world cup.

But however big or grand the tent you will eventually settle with is, it is still different from the sturdy stone walls of your bedroom at home. It may be a bit unsettling for beginners when they're inside the tent, and strong winds suddenly start attacking them. At this point, the tent, of course, will feel flimsy compared to a solid structure. Another reality in camping that you will have to face is that you will be at the mercy of the elements, nature, and some other wildlife.

So if you are indeed going to sleep in your car or tent,

better check and try your setup first before going ahead on your trip. A good night's sleep is a requirement for a safer drive home, so choose wisely.

Prepare to Disconnect

Let us not forget the internet and connectivity, of course. Even though we are very connected nowadays with free Wi-Fi connections that can be found in every neighborhood coffee shop, which is not always the case when you are out in the great outdoors.

Though some cell services will boast the widest coverage, some will still have patches where there is absolutely no internet connection. If you are planning to go for an extended car camping trip where you would need to have a working internet connection, prepare a Wi-Fi booster, or again, book a slot in a well-equipped campsite with full hookups.

Upsetting for some and reinvigorating for others to realize, the world does not revolve around a single person, no matter how poetic it might be. You will notice that the world does keep on spinning without you even if you are gone for 2 weeks. So sit back and jump out from the hamster wheel of humanity once in a while to recharge. It will do you good mentally and physically - I promise.

If you think you can disconnect and go off the grid completely, do this simple experiment.

Buy one of those old late '90s to early 2000s phones where you can only call and receive text messages. Leave your smartphone in your home for the whole day. It won't be that hard when you are working as you will have access to the internet while you are in the office via your computer or laptop. But the feeling of not having anyone calling or chatting you up randomly is exhilarating and freeing. It's almost like an adventure in itself.

I, unfortunately, found out the hard way that I was a bit dependent on my phone and gadgets when my phone decided to take a dip in the river with me. I had to go phoneless for 2 months. Not having anything to fiddle with while in line for my morning coffee is sheer torture. I kept reaching for my pocket and found myself squeezing my old brick phone absentmindedly.

Food Changes

You will not have the same amount of space or even equipment to prepare the meals you are used to at home.

At the very least, we car campers can have the luxury of warm cooked food. Although it may not be a full course meal, it will still be hearty if you pick up a few one-pot recipes along the way. But if you are not the cooking type, instant ramen will be your friend. Try to see if you can fit a propane stove or a grill inside your trunk, so you will always have hot water no matter what.

Types of Vehicles That are Best for Car Camping

If there's a will, there's a way. That's my grandmother's favorite saying.

You can often hear that SUVs are perfect if you want to go car camping, but frankly, you can use any type of vehicle for car camping. I myself have used my old and trusty second-hand Honda hatchback for a year before I have saved enough to purchase a bigger, also second-hand, SUV.

But to properly be able to experience all the comforts car camping can bring, SUVs will be the way to go. Why an SUV, you might ask? With my Honda hatchback, I was limited to paved roads and campsites nearer to the city. It was perfect for the city too. But my SUV wins in the backcountry roads, hands down.

Although, there's really nothing wrong with smaller vehicles, so if you have a perfectly capable sedan or hatchback with you, go ahead and use it! Just keep in mind to know your car's limits. Like if it's an old faithful, try not to go over dirt roads or go in the boondocks. You might get stuck, and you will end up needing to call a tow company in the middle of nowhere.

But all in all, the main reason I chose to buy an SUV is because I wanted a bigger trunk space so I can bring my new tents with me. And I also wanted to try camping off-grid. I needed something that could tackle dirt roads with no problem.

These bigger vehicles offer an added ground clearance as well as payload. The right model also has enough towing capacity to haul cargo and your friends, making it perfect for family trips and off-grid camping.

An SUV is a sport utility vehicle. Through the years, they have grown in popularity, and manufacturers have been quick to answer to the demands of consumers. I've compiled a shorter version of my notes and made them more legible to help you out with your vehicle choices.

Kia Soul - $19,190 base price

Cargo space:

62.1 cubic feet with the seats down

24.2 cubic feet with the seats upright

Ground clearance: 6.7 inches

This subcompact SUV might not be treated as an SUV by many because of its size, hence the category subcompact and its price tag. It is the cheapest starting price you can find for any subcompact SUV. It's a FWD or a front wheel drive, so you might meet some problems if you plan to bring it on an off-road trip.

Subaru Outback - $26,795 base price

Cargo space:

78 cubic feet with the seats down

33 cubic feet with seats upright

Ground clearance: 9.5 inches

I settled with this, by the way. The dealer called it the Swiss army knife of cars - what can I say, I get persuaded easily. It does great in the urban setting, but it shines when it's taking on backcountry roads with its 4 wheel drive. It has collapsible roof racks as well as wide doors that will make loading and unloading a breeze. The popularity of this car for camping conveniently makes it easy to find the perfect and compatible rooftop tent for your camping needs.

Chrysler Pacifica - $39,000 base price for 4 wheel drives

Cargo space:

140.5 cubic feet with the second and third-row seats folded down

32.3 cubic feet with the seats upright

Ground clearance: 5.1 inches

Winning the most number of awards a minivan could ever have 5 years in a row, this is probably one of the most spacious on this list. A large inflatable mattress could easily fit inside since both the second and third-row seats fold down to the floor. Although the ground clearance is not that high compared to the SUVs in this room, with its hauling (3,600 pounds) and storage capacity, this car would be a match made in heaven for campers who are looking for serious storage spaces in their vehicle.

Jeep Gladiator - $33,545 base price

Cargo space: 35.5 cubic feet with the tailgate closed

Ground clearance: 11.66 inches

This was a strong contender for me, just because of its name. I feel like every time I touch the hood of this thing, I will recite Russel Crowe's monologue in Gladiator. Anyway, this mid-sized pickup truck can tow a whopping 7,650 pounds, so it will be easy to drag a towable along with this thing. The roof and doors can be taken out, leaving you with a cool Jurassic Park-looking vehicle where you can see the stars easily in the night sky or a t-rex about to swallow you whole.

Ford Bronco Sport - $27,265 base price

Cargo space:

65.2 cubic feet with the seats down

32.5 cubic feet with the upright

Ground clearance: 7.9 inches

With a boxy shape that makes it easy for you to load and unload larger gears, this compact crossover SUV's interior is definitely roomy. The dealer said that 2 mountain bikes can be easily stored inside. Aside from the storage, it looks like Ford wants to make this compact crossover a car for camping enthusiasts by adding in a ton of outdoor and handy features like Molle straps and bottle openers.

Toyota Land Cruiser - $85,415 base price

Cargo space:

82.8 cubic feet when all seats are folded down

41.4 cubic feet when third-row seats are folded

16.1 cubic feet with all seats upright

Ground clearance: 8.5 inches

The land cruiser has a special place in my heart because this is the first SUV I have ever bought. Toyota Land Cruisers have been around for so long that my dad even had one when he was in university - I think they started manufacturing these in the 1950s, making these Toyota's longest-produced vehicles. In some versions, the third row splits and folds to the side, giving you more storage room. Some editions, however, remove the third row altogether. While the storage capacity and interior might not be the best, the Land Cruiser shines in its off-road capabilities.

Honda Passport - $37,870 base price

Cargo space:

41.2 cubic feet behind the second row of seats

77.9 cubic feet with all the seats down

Ground clearance: 7.5 inches

It might not be a Land Rover, but the Honda Passport is definitely fit for the outdoors. The insides are roomy, and you will have no problem fitting it with inflatable mattresses for a good night's sleep. But if you prefer to sleep outside, rooftop tents are a good alternative too. You'll have to purchase mods for it to make it more camping-ready, though. Not to worry - there are companies like Jsport's that can fit you with all the necessary gear you need, from skid plates to roof racks.

Land Rover Defender - $57,800 base price

Cargo space:

Three-row Defender:

10.7 cubic feet behind the third-row seats

34.6 cubic feet behind the second-row seats

69 cubic feet all rear seat folded

Two-door Defender :

15.6 cubic feet with the second-row seats folded

58.3 cubic feet when all rear seats are folded.

Ground clearance: 11.5 inches

If we are going to discuss the Toyota Land Cruiser, then we must also include the Land Rover in our list. Even though both cars have very good off-road reputations, I feel like the Land Rover Defender has more oomph to it. The whole vehicle is a perfect blend of that luxurious and rugged look that just screams, "Look at me! I am King!" It comes with a lot of options that can let you customize the Defender into your perfect camping buddy.

Dodge Durango

Cargo Space:

85.1 cubic feet when all the rear seats are down

43.3 cubic feet with the third row folded and

17.3 cubic feet with the third-row seats upright

Ground clearance: 8.1 inches

There are a few versions of the Durango out there, but the 4 wheel drive Durango R/T Tow N' Go is the one that caught my eye. With a towing capacity of 8,700 pounds, hauling your jet skis won't be a problem. Inside, it has ample space once all rear seats have been folded down, but I found that the bucket seats in the first 2 rows are already comfy enough for a nap.

Chapter 2: Defining Stealth (Urban) Camping and Legalities

With all my words pushing you to do car camping or to actually sleep in your car, did you know that some laws actually stop you from sleeping in your car? Different states have different laws when it comes to overnight camping, so wherever you go, do extensive research first.

Anyway, when I started sleeping in my car, I was lucky I had someone knowledgeable about all this by my side to hold my hand. In the city, I was in, overnight parking in rest stops is illegal, so I had to resort to stealth camping. Sometimes, I can park at a friend's or an acquaintance's driveway - but through the following months, I did make up a mental list of places where I can sleep safely for the night.

It might not seem much, especially if you are not living in your car. But plans do change at the last minute, whether intentional or accidental. And even if you are a seasoned camper traveling in an RV, a van, or any kind of vehicle for that matter, you will find yourself sleeping in your chosen vehicle. A lot.

Think about it: if you are traveling or living in your vehicle for a long time, you will probably have valuables with you. And no, I don't mean boxes of money and jewelry. I am talking about your phones, laptops, and gadgets. Even your roof rack, bikes, and tents can be stolen. I even heard of people getting their side-view mirrors stolen. So, it pays to be very careful and to know a lot about the environment you are planning to stay in.

But what exactly is stealth camping? I'd like to think it's camping undetected, whether it is for safety reasons or boondocking. But generally, if you do your research on the great Web, there are two major divides in stealth camping. The first involves our topic for this book - camping in your car - while the second is camping in a place where basically no one camps in (kind of like boondocking). The first is a common occurrence for people living the van life or the car life. The second is more familiar for the thrill-seekers, the long-distance cyclists, and the survivalists.

But why do stealth camping? Some people don't have the luxury of staying in hotels and such. Not all people choose to do stealth camping - some are forced to do it out of necessity. But let's start with the brighter side of stealth camping.

For the hardcore nature lovers, stealth camping in the wilderness gives them the freedom and the solitude they can't feel when they're in a campsite; plus, it's convenient. Picture this: you just hiked through two mountains today. You are tired, and you've just found a perfect clearing where you can rest for the night. The campsite is hours away. Would you want to walk miles again just to reach the designated campsite? No! You know your limits, and you need to rest, so you set up camp in the middle of nowhere. That right there is stealth camping.

Others take the more spontaneous approach or what I call "the explorer" method. I had friends like this when I was still backpacking through Southeast Asia. We had our flight tickets all ready for the next day, but my friend heard of a great festival happening in the neighboring town the next night. He then proceeded to drive all the way there, stealth camped the night and missed our flight the next day.

As you can see, it's the spontaneity and freedom that makes stealth camping addicting for some. It's like the "I can sleep anywhere standing up" concept but on steroids. Of course, there is another less fun facet of stealth camping - the "all my plans went down the drain" and "I don't know where to sleep" kind of stealth camping.

For some, stealth camping is a necessity when traveling long distances. A lot of aspects will lead to stealth camping in parks, mall parking lots, and fast-food chain parking lots. Some do it because, again, their plans didn't go the way they planned. But most do stealth camping because it is essentially free camping - so long as you do not get caught illegally parking on a roadside (you'll have to pay a fine). This is especially true for travelers on a low budget. Motels and hotels are pricey, and even staying the night in a campsite can fetch a hefty sum.

One thing is for sure: stealth camping can be a fun way to camp. It will be a memorable experience for first-timers, I can assure you. For whatever reason you approach stealth camping, you will need to be very careful. I've had a friend who decided to sleep in his van near an abandoned farm, only to be woken up by dogs barking and the owner peering in with a very bright torchlight holding on to a shotgun. Don't worry - they shared a beer on the man's front porch after he nearly peed himself from fright. But be forewarned that not all things end bright and cheery - some owners will shoot first before asking questions.

So to stealth camp, first, you need to know how to stealth camp. If you are going to stealth camp in the wilderness, no matter how much you love your peace and quiet and your withdrawal from the connected world, you do need to tell someone back home where you are going. It's very dangerous going off-grid without telling anyone. Bring with you a satellite phone at all times and tell people where you plan to stay.

Next, you need to know where you plan to camp - at least roughly. There is a divide if you are planning to go stealth camping in an urban setting versus if you are going to go boondocking, but looking for the right, legal, and safe place to camp applies to both types of stealth camping.

Stealth camping in nature is essentially boondocking too. You are thereby avoiding the well-trodden trails and paths in campsites and national parks in favor of going off-grid. A few people will push for a "hiding from the world" kind of stealth camping - that means literally hiding, making it harder for authorities to find you in case there's an accident. I don't recommend that at all if you are a beginner. If you want peace and quiet, some national parks and state parks can offer you that easily.

When stealth camping in the wild, there are a few things that you would need to do. You have to assess the space first. Is it safe? Are there reports of bear sightings? How fast can you reach the trail again? Then park your car facing where you would want to leave in case of an emergency. You should aim to reach your prospective campsite early when the sun is still high up in the sky, so you can clearly see and survey the area.

The same goes for dirt roads, even if you drive a 4 wheel drive. If the road looks like it hasn't been used since the dawn of time, get out of your car and survey the road on foot first to avoid getting your vehicle stuck. Walk around the perimeter and stay for an hour or two, checking your surroundings for signs of dangerous wildlife without pulling any of your gears out. When all is clear, then you can set up your camp.

If you find yourself near a body of water, camp away or above the water and check the water levels as well as the weather report regularly. Sometimes they also open dams which can cause the water to rise quickly - this happens even on clear days, so check with the state websites for announcements too.

Urban Camping

When stealth camping in an urban setting, however, you will find that the stealth part is really very necessary. Look around and research the neighborhood or environment that you are in. Check the crime rates. A safe spot should be:

Well-lit - avoid areas that are dark and downtrodden.

Dim areas usually have higher crime rates. CCTVs are also a welcome sight.

Clean - if there are trash and broken glasses everywhere, something unsightly might have happened, and it might happen to you too. When your life is at stake, you can never be too cautious.

Level ground - park in an area that is not on an incline. Engage your hand brakes too. You don't want the car to start rolling down while you are inside asleep.

And when you do park somewhere to sleep, cover all windows so no one can see you sleeping inside. This also aims to protect your valuables from hungry eyes. If you have removable roof racks or bikes tied to the tops or sides of your car, keep them very secured or bolted into place. Otherwise, you can try to bring them inside your vehicle. When stealth camping, your state of awareness needs to be constantly high because everything can change in a minute.

If it sounds kind of scary, do not fear - a lot of campers really do sleep in their cars. In fact, there are tons of locations all across the country where you can park and stay for the night. There are also apps out there specifically catered to people who are looking for overnight parking choices, like the infamous Allstays app for overnight parking at Walmart.

And to help you out, here's a small list of where it is typically allowed to park and sleep overnight.

Walmart parking lots

Urban legend says that the owner of Walmart is an enthusiastic RVer, so he allows his fellow camping enthusiasts to use the parking lot for boondocking. But the rules for overnight parking in their stores depend on the state and the individual stores themselves, so it would be best to call ahead and ask the store manager before assuming anything. They also post signs everywhere telling you whether overnight parking is not allowed.

Boondocking in a 24-hour Walmart is preferred by a lot of people because it's well-lit and is usually monitored. A single girl sleeping in her car would sleep a lot better under the lights and CCTV cameras.

Other big-box store parking lots

When you drive past your local chain stores at night,

you might see a congregation of RVs and campers parked for the night. Most of these offer free overnight parking, but again, it will depend on store management. To be sure, ask first before you settle in. Here's a list of chain stores that are popular with boondockers:

Walmart

Kmart

Denny's

Lowes

Bass Pro Shops

IHOP

Target

KFC

24-hour grocery stores like Safeway and WinCo

Holiday Inn

Marriott Inn

Cabela's

Menards

Home Depot

Camping World

Costco

Visitor centers

What a lot of people don't know is that visitor centers in cities or near tourist destinations would usually let people stay for the night. The parking area is usually left unoccupied during the nighttime and can provide campers access to basic utilities like a bathroom and fresh water.

Truck stops and rest areas

Most truck stops allow boondocking, but they're a dark and scary place most of the time as there is minimal security. Also, the trucks are huge, and I feel like I would be squashed to death parked in the middle of two 18 wheelers. The traffic can be noisy with all the trucks and semis coming and going at all hours of the night, so be sure to bring earplugs with you if you want a good night's sleep.

Hotel and motel parking lots

Try to find hotel and motel parking lots that are mostly empty at night. I found that major chains won't mind that much if you park in their empty lots for the night.

Trailheads

A lot of trails are used for backpacking trips, so it is not unusual to find a lot of campers staying overnight at the trailheads.

Casino parking lots

This is a great option if you are driving through Las Vegas. Casinos are open 24/7, and most patrons will stay inside for days, so staying overnight shouldn't be a problem.

Small towns and gas stations

Some small towns will offer free overnight parking to guests to boost their foot traffic. They're hoping you might stay longer and buy a couple of local products. Small gas stations in the middle of nowhere will also offer free overnight parking. On both sites, remember to ask permission first.

In cases of emergencies, in a pinch, schools and church parking lots will do too. Most will allow overnight parking if you just ask. Another thing you could do is go to the local police station directly and ask them politely where you could park overnight legally. This is better than chancing and parking somewhere only to find the local police force knocking on your window telling you to move.

Another important aspect is your actions while stealth camping. And no, I'm not talking about your environmental footprint - that is important too, but it's under ethics, not here. The main thing in stealth camping is that you are hidden, and you want to be hidden. Your actions shouldn't give away the fact that you are sleeping in your car, especially in an urban setting, even if you are parked there legally. It's for your own safety too!

Do not set up camp. Parking someplace overnight doesn't mean you can bring out your tents or sleep in your rooftop tent. You will have to squeeze inside your car, so you have to pack accordingly. The 80-something cubic feet in your rear doesn't mean you need to pack your whole house in there - reserve a space for you to sleep in, always. It also doesn't mean that you can prop up your propane stove outside to enjoy the cool night air, as tempting as it may sound, and cook your meals in the middle of the Walmart parking lot. Do not be obnoxious and play loud music, thereby disturbing other shoppers and campers.

Being considerate to others and maintaining a low profile is the key to safe and successful stealth camping. Not only will you be keeping yourself safe, but you are also doing other campers a favor. By putting your best foot forward, you are adding to the good name of campers everywhere. Remember: free overnight parking is a privilege earned, not a right.

State Laws on Urban Camping

Listed below is my cheat sheet on state laws on overnight parking. The laws and regulations can change, so it's better to call ahead to make sure.

Alabama: No overnight parking in rest stops.

Alaska: Laws may vary in different cities.

Arizona: Overnight parking allowed in rest stops (camping outside of your vehicle is prohibited).

Arkansas: Overnight parking allowed in rest stops (camping outside of your vehicle is prohibited).

California: No overnight parking in rest stops (there's an 8-hour limit). There are designated parking lots for overnight parking.

Colorado: No overnight parking in rest stops. There are designated parking lots for overnight parking.

Connecticut: No overnight parking in rest stops. Laws may vary in different cities.

Delaware: No overnight parking in rest stops (there's a 4-hour limit). Laws may vary in different cities.

Florida: No overnight parking in rest stops (there's a 3-hour limit). Laws may vary in different cities.

Georgia: No overnight parking in rest stops.

Hawaii: No overnight parking in rest stops. Sleeping inside your car is prohibited.

Idaho: Overnight parking allowed in rest stops (there's a 10-hour limit; camping outside of your vehicle is prohibited).

Illinois: No overnight parking in rest stops (there's a 3-hour limit).

Indiana: No overnight parking in rest stops.

Iowa: Overnight parking allowed in rest stops during emergencies.

Kansas: Overnight parking allowed in rest stops for 1 night.

Kentucky: No overnight parking in rest stops (there's a 4-hour limit).

Louisiana: No overnight parking in rest stops.

Maine: No overnight parking in rest stops.

Maryland: No overnight parking in rest stops (there's a

3-hour limit).

Massachusetts: No overnight parking in rest stops.

Michigan: No overnight parking in rest stops (there's a 4-hour limit).

Minnesota: No overnight parking in rest stops (there's a 4-hour limit).

Mississippi: No overnight parking in rest stops (camping outside of your vehicle is prohibited).

Missouri: No overnight parking in rest stops (camping outside of your vehicle is prohibited).

Montana: No overnight parking in rest stops (camping outside of your vehicle is prohibited).

Nebraska: No overnight parking in rest stops (there's a 10-hour limit).

Nevada: Overnight parking allowed in rest stops (there's a 24-hour limit) (camping outside of your vehicle is allowed).

New Hampshire: No overnight parking in rest stops (there's a 4-hour limit).

New Jersey: Overnight parking allowed in designated areas (camping outside of your vehicle is prohibited).

New Mexico: Overnight parking allowed in rest stops (there's a 24-hour limit) (camping outside of your vehicle is prohibited)

New York: No overnight parking in rest stops (there's a 3-hour limit).

North Carolina: No overnight parking in rest stops (there's a 4-hour limit).

North Dakota: Overnight parking allowed in rest stops (camping outside of your vehicle is prohibited).

Ohio: No overnight parking in rest stops (there's a 3-hour limit). There are designated parking lots for overnight parking.

Oklahoma: Overnight parking allowed in rest stops (camping outside of your vehicle is prohibited).

Oregon: Overnight parking allowed in rest stops (there's a 12-hour limit; camping outside of your vehicle is prohibited).

Pennsylvania: No overnight parking in rest stops (there's a 2-hour limit).

Rhode Island: Overnight parking allowed in rest stops (camping outside of your vehicle is prohibited).

South Carolina: No overnight parking in rest stops.

South Dakota: No overnight parking in rest stops (there's a 4-hour limit).

Tennessee: No overnight parking in rest stops (there's a 2-hour limit).

Texas: Overnight parking allowed in rest stops (there's a 24-hour limit) (camping outside of your vehicle is prohibited).

Utah: No overnight parking in rest stops.

Vermont: No overnight parking in rest stops.

Virginia: No overnight parking in rest stops.

Washington: Overnight parking allowed in rest stops (there's an 8-hour limit) (camping outside of your vehicle is prohibited).

West Virginia: Overnight parking allowed in rest stops (camping outside of your vehicle is prohibited).

Wisconsin: No overnight parking in rest stops.

Wyoming: Overnight parking allowed in rest stops (camping outside of your vehicle is prohibited).

Chapter 3: How to Plan Your Trip: Gearing Up

You can never be too prepared for a camping trip. Even though bringing and camping in a car would help a lot in getting you out of sticky situations, like running out of food or forgetting the stove, it would still be a huge bummer if you have to go down to the town for every single item you forgot.

So what do you need and how do you plan your trip? Provided you have already planned out where to go and camp, research the places you plan to go to and get all the reservations and/or permits. Check your vehicle and see if it's in tip-top condition. If not, have it serviced.

Then, take stock of your vehicle's storage space and start thinking about the gear you will be needing. I would like to say, "Don't buy too much gear; you won't be able to use them all." But I'm guilty of hoarding gear. I think I have around 10 tents in my third bedroom as I type this. I probably should rent them out, but I'm too fuzzy with my things.

But first, let us talk about the essentials of every camping trip, car camping or not. These "10 essentials" were compiled by a Seattle-based organization called The Mountaineers in the 1930s. It was later formalized in the 1970s and is written with the wisdom and experience of hundreds of outdoors skills instructors.

When preparing your essential gear, you should ask yourself two questions. With the things you brought with you, can you prevent emergencies and respond to one should it happen? Can you survive a night or more outdoors with your items? Depending on the nature of your trip, the equipment can vary, but the first 7 in this list are non-negotiables for me. Keeping these essentials with you at all times can save your life in case of emergencies.

Navigation

These 5 are essentials: maps, GPS, altimeter watch, a compass, and a PLB or a personal locator beacon. Any type of navigation device, satellite communicator, and satellite phone, and extra batteries.

Map

Learn to read physical maps - it's a skill you will be needing even in the modern world, especially if you want to start camping. A basic topographic map should also be in your backpack when you camp and hike in ridges, canyons, and mountains.

Here's a tip: Download the Gaia GPS app and keep an offline map of the site you want to visit on your phone in case you find yourself somewhere without a connection.

Compass

Even though most watches and phones now have compasses, you should still have a standard compass in your backpack. It doesn't rely on batteries, and it's as light as a feather. It shouldn't take too much space in your pack.

GPS Device

A new addition to the family. A GPS device can pinpoint your exact location on a map. There are devices sold in the market specifically designed for outdoor use, meaning they can withstand shock and water and have a longer battery life. An alternative would be a smartphone app, but keep in mind that most phones right now are still too fragile for outdoor use - they're not waterproof, and the battery life is a joke. Take necessary precautions like an extra battery pack, shockproof cases, and a matching lanyard if you do plan to use your phone.

Altimeter Watch

This device can measure air pressure using a barometric sensor. It can help you keep track of your progress and location at any given time.

PLB, also known as personal locator beacon or satellite messenger: During times of emergency, a PLB can be used to alert rescuers of your position using GPS for rescue. Some can also work as a messaging device in locations where there's no cell service.

Survival Gear

Headlamp and Extra Batteries

A good choice for backcountry camping is a headlamp, leaving your hands free to do other more important things.

Sun Protection

Sunscreen, sunglasses, UV blocking clothes

First Aid

You can pack your own first aid kit, but you can easily find pre-packed kits in lots of camping stores and even in pharmacies. A good first aid kit should include adhesive bandages in different sizes, treatment for blisters, gauze pads, micropore tapes, disinfecting or antibacterial ointment, pain medications, and nitrile gloves. Also, try to find a concise guide tackling how to treat various medical emergencies.

Knife and Repair Kit

Knives are irreplaceable in camping as they can be

used in various situations, from food preparation to making kindling for a fire. A Swiss army knife is also good. Aside from the knife, also carry with you a simple repair kit in case of emergencies. "If all else fails, use duct tape," my dad used to say. A roll of duct tape, cords, and zip ties will do well for the most part.

Fire

Anything that can produce fire; matches, lighters, or tinder. If you plan to bring matches, make sure they are not the ones you can usually find in groceries or supermarkets. They should be waterproof or are stored in a waterproof container. Fire starters must also be packed. These should ignite quickly. A few examples are dry tinder, lint trappings, heat nuggets, candles, and priming paste.

Life Essentials

Shelter

Aside from your bigger tent, an emergency shelter must be carried with you at all times. A lightweight bivy sack or tent should work well in providing you shelter from rain and wind in case you get lost or stranded.

Extra Food

Pack extra portions of light food, enough for a couple or more days in case of emergencies. These should not require heat or preparation and should have a long shelf life. A few good examples are dried fruits, jerky, energy bars, and nuts.

Extra Water

Fresh water is crucial for survival, but it is heavy. If you are hiking or camping where there's a nearby water source, consider bringing along some kind of water treatment gadget, like a handy water purifier or a filter. Bring a collapsible bottle with you so you can fill it up as you go. Remember: person would need half a liter per hour when doing fairly moderate activities.

Extra Clothes

When out in nature, weather conditions can change almost immediately. It might get cold suddenly, or it might suddenly rain. Pack extra clothes that you can easily take off or layer.

So, onto my own favorite part in any camping trip: the gear. I "ooh and aah" every time I see new gear being introduced. I do try to keep myself from buying it, but I end up thinking and dreaming about me using it. So, in the end, I do end up buying it.

Optional Gear

Below is a list of things you can consider bringing with you when car camping. It's not a definite list - you can add and subtract things from this to tailor it to your own needs - but these are the basics, more or less.

Sleeping Pad or a Mattress Pad

A sleeping pad or a mattress pad will bring you the cushioning and comfort you'll need when sleeping. It can be used both in the vehicle or inside the tent. It can also provide extra insulation during the colder months. And if you are using a tent, a sleeping pad will provide a cushion from the hard ground, ensuring a good night's sleep. An alternative would be an inflatable mattress.

Tent

This is really optional. If you want to go minimal in your car camping endeavors and your vehicle is big enough to accommodate you fully reclined, then you won't need a tent. Just a pad would do. But if you do need a tent, there are a lot of styles out there. I personally like the bigger one where I can walk around and stand up inside. It's temporary, I know because I go camping for a maximum of 2 nights during the weekends, but I want it to be absolutely cozy when I'm inside.

Sleeping Bags

In the colder months, you absolutely need a sleeping bag. It can provide extra warmth and comfort - plus, it keeps your toes from freezing. Be sure to check the temperature rating on them and choose the one that would suit the conditions you will use them in.

Pillows and Blankets

There are inflatable pillows specifically made for camping, but they might be a little expensive. So, the pillows from your own bedroom will fork just fine. Bring one and also a couple of blankets for extra warmth.

Lamps

I have already tackled headlamps in the "10 essentials", but bringing along other lamps will be useful. I mean, who doesn't need extra illumination, right? Nights in the outdoors are absolutely pitch black, and your actions might probably be limited with just a headlamp on. So, bring along with you a couple of battery-powered LED lamps that you can hang around the campsite and in your car. It would provide a festive and more welcoming appearance - some even bring fairy lights!

Camp Chairs and Foldable Tables

A camp chair or 2 will make a good addition to your camping collection. They're foldable, lightweight, and are easy to transport. Just be sure to hold on to them when the wind starts picking up - I always end up running after mine. Foldable tables are a godsend too. I mean, you can use a rock as a table and chair, but you'd probably have back pains afterward. With a folding table, you'd have more counter space where you can prepare and eat your meals in comfort.

Kitchen Gear

Reserve the dried nuts and the tough jerkies for your emergency supply because camping doesn't mean you have to eat nuts and berries like a squirrel all weekend. Packing along a few basic camp kitchen gear can get you started on some nice hearty dishes. Bring along some cutlery like plates and bowls. A cast iron pan, a small pot, and a Dutch oven are also a good option if you plan to bring a propane stove. You can also use a small electric grill if you plan to camp in a full hookup campsite or some propane-powered ones when boondocking. Bring along a water jug and a cooler too.

If you plan to pack and cook raw food, reusable ice packs can keep your food cool and not swimming in ice water by the time nightfall comes. Here's a small checklist of some kitchen utensils that you might consider packing:

Coolers and reusable ice packs

Water jugs and water bottles

Grills or over-the-fire grates - most campgrounds have their own grills, but it is unsanitary to use the campground grills. So try to bring your own grates if you plan on using them.

Wooden spoons and spatulas

Tongs

Can and bottle openers

Metal skewers - for BBQing stuff over the campfire. We are aiming for sustainability here.

Bowls, plates, and various other cutleries

A small chopping board

Propane stove or grill

Saving Storage Space

I think I told you before: I'm a hoarder - you should see my house. My third bedroom is a no-man zone. I can't bear to open it unless I need to. But! I am proud to say that I have grown pretty good at packing light. It's a skill, I know. My proudest skill is that I can squeeze 2 weeks' worth of items in one luggage bag.

But I wasn't like this before. In fact, years ago, I often found myself standing in front of my rear car door, arms akimbo, hair all over the place, wondering if I should just give up and lie on the wooden decking for the rest of the day.

So here are some of my top tips on how you can maximize the storage in your car. Hint: it's like playing Tetris.

Separate things by size and use.

Small things tend to get lost in the clutter of the larger bags. Group the small items by use. For example, small kitchen utensils should be in one pack, and electronics that you are not going to use until you get to your campsite in another. Items like your phone, keys, lamps, and maps should be next to you, so you don't have to look like an ostrich diving into the back of your car looking for the headlamp and lamps when the sunlight is fading fast.

Important items should be stored next to you or in the glove compartment. Your pack with the "10 essentials" should be in the backseat. Take stock of your valuables too. If you have a small safe, keep it chained to somewhere in the interior of the car that is not easily visible when you look through the window. You don't want a removable safe that a thief could just scurry away with.

Pro tip: Keep your car key secure too. There are "under the car" key cases that can be bought. If you are forgetful like me, keep a spare key in there, so you don't have to get locked out of your car in the middle of the trip. It would just ruin the trip, and everyone would get mad at you - trust me, I'm speaking from experience.

Get a cargo carrier.

If your car is on the smaller side, a great way of adding more storage space is by adding a cargo carrier on your roof or to your rear. This is especially useful if the car rear is also your sleeping quarters. Just make sure these are bolted or properly secured to your roof, and they have security locks.

There are tons of anti-theft cargo carriers available in the market. Some attach to the roof, some to the rear of the car. Keep the bulkier equipment up there, like the tents and kitchen camping gear.

Consider a cargo hammock.

A cargo hammock is great when you want to store items in the ceiling of your car. But you might find that things may shift in the hammock while you are driving, so try not to place heavy things inside while you are still driving. A bumpy road or a sudden stop, and you might have a pillow bouncing off the back of your head. Otherwise, it's a great option for additional storage, especially if you plan to sleep and live in your car.

Use the side door storage and get "behind the seat" organizers.

Did you know that the cubby holes in your car door's are surprisingly spacious? When you live or camp in your car, every little space is prime real estate, so stuff them full of other things and the smaller packs. Also, get some of those seat organizers that you can hang at the back of your car seats.

Get cargo bins.

Cargo bins can help you stay organized. In fact, you won't need to get one of those ultra-fancy cargo bins they sell for camping - even the simple plastic storage boxes you can easily get from Ikea will work wonderfully. I love those transparent boxes because I can find the stuff I need faster.

Load the cargo bins into the car first and cushion them all around with the packs and bags to keep them secure throughout the ride. Pro Tip: Label your containers accordingly.

Chapter 4: Car Camping With Kids

I used to hate going to campsites filled with screaming kids. Wait, in fact, I still hate it. Imagine kids running around causing havoc all over, and their parents just sitting there in their camping chairs stuck in their AstroTurf lawn in front of their RVs holding their beers, saying stuff like "kids will be kids." Ugh, no. Having kids running around destroying public and private property is not cute. Some parents even have the gall to blog about it. "My baby boy just started playing with a historical artifact in a museum - the attendant was looking at us, but it's their fault for not adding a playground in here."

But my sister has 2 kids, and I grudgingly admit, I spoil them rotten, and I'd like to believe that they're some of the most well-behaved kids I have ever seen. Maybe. They could simply be scared of me, but I'd like to believe they're in awe of me. Anyway, I taught them the right way to camp and what not to do when camping. But then again, kids will still be kids. I know; I'm parroting their words. But they are just little balls of energy that need to be contained and pacified most of the time, especially if you plan to bring them with you in car camping trips.

And I understand it's hard to bring kids' car camping. When my sister dumps the nieces with me when they go abroad for a few days because of work, I bring them car camping. Through the years, I'd like to think they're veterans now. The eldest even carries and packs her own stuff (insert proud aunt moment here).

Below is a list I've compiled that can hopefully help you successfully and peacefully camp in your car with kids.

Make Lists

Lists will save your day.

List down everything in an app or in a large yellow legal. No matter how many brain booster vitamins you take every day, there is no way you can keep track of everything.

When you decide to go car camping with kids during their breaks, start making the list early on so you won't forget a thing. Camping by yourself is relatively easy, but bringing along kids who are still developing their views of the world and their sense of danger is doubly difficult. You need to make sure you have your gear and that they have theirs, plus that the food will last for everyone in your family. You need to make up activities that can occupy your kids' time - and hope to tire them out so they'll fall in a deep and long sleep until the next morning.

Plan Ahead

Pack days in advance.

Pack the items you are not using in your everyday lives first, like camping gear and clothes. As you get nearer to D-day, load the camping gear into your car a day in advance so you can focus your attention packing the perishables on the day itself.

Bigger is Better

The bigger your vehicle, the better.

There is no way you, your partner, and even the kids will fit in a sedan, so consider getting an SUV, a van, or something bigger. A cramped car is no way to enjoy your car camping trip.

Camp Nearby

Unfortunately, the age of your kids is in direct relation to how far away you can go from the city. If your kids are younger, it is better to choose campsites that are closer to where you live or closer to the city. Save the cross-country trips when your kids are older, more responsible, and would need less taking care of. Camping near your house also has its benefits. You can get to your destination quicker, even if you meet unexpected delays and arrive at your campsite well past your scheduled arrival. This way, you can still have time to unpack and set up camp before sundown.

Buddy System

Have a camping buddy.

Camping with friends and families with other kids is a great way to enjoy your car camping trips. It has two major benefits, the way I see it. One, you would have more adults around to help keep an eye on the kids. Two, you can have more time to relax when more adults are watching over the kids. Therefore, there is less stress, and you can have someone to talk to.

Chore Time

Give your kids a task.

Giving your kids something to do instead of just waiting around and watching the adults set up camp is going to be productive. Basically, have your kids do something other than simply staring out the window of your car. Have them help you gather kindling to the fire or hold on to the sides of the tent. Kids love it if they feel like they're doing something important. That attitude wanes, though, as they get older. Depending on the kid, a sulky and irritated adolescent or teen on a camping trip is as worse as having a baby on a trip.

Be Organized

Keep track of things.

Be organized and clean up as you go. Things go where they need to go. Clean dishes after dinner. Less mess also means less clean-up, and you will find that you will have more time for more activities. Teach your kids to pick up after themselves, if not in the house, at least during the camping trip.

Play Time

Let the kids play.

And no, I don't mean let them run around the place disturbing other campers. Please be considerate and let us treat each other with respect. If you want your kids to run around like hooligans, rent an estate far out in the

English countryside. What I meant was to let them play and don't be so strict. If they get their overalls dirty, fine. Camping is supposed to be fun anyway, and dirty too. Just make sure their hands are clean during meal times, and they brush their teeth at least twice a day. Wet wipes are your best friends during camping.

Chapter 5: Finding Your Campsite

Now, you may be thinking that I've already covered this part in the previous sections of this book, but that was all about stealth camping - or what I love to call stealth parking - at least most of the time. And although stealth camping in the wild or what others call boondocking was already discussed, I feel like I haven't gone in-depth on where you can actually camp in the wild.

Boondocking is kind of a catch-all term for any kind of free camping in the wild. Usually, it is also a form of dry camping or a form of camping without any hookups. To make it clearer, dry camping is camping without any provided access for fresh water, electricity, and sewage. Partial hookups mean that you are provided with only one or two hookups out of the three. Full hookups mean you can camp with all three amenities.

Below are sites where you can experience different kinds of camping. For most, you have to pay a fee to camp, but there are also choices where you can camp for free. In these free sites, you are expected to do boondocking or dispersed camping - as the government agencies like to call it. So be prepared to bring fresh water, mini generators, a trowel, and waste bags during your stay, and remember to confirm your reservations first before you drive out.

Campgrounds - Free to $50 Per Night

(Dry Camping to Partial Hookups)

Most rustic out of the three choices listed here, these sites are usually located in the national and state parks. Although some of the more popular campgrounds might have hookups and amenities, it would be better to prepare for dry camping when you plan to camp here. However, the sites are bigger, and you would also find yourself surrounded by nature more often than not. I think it is also worth noting that most roads you will tackle to get to the campgrounds are going to be unpaved, but a 4-wheel drive might be able to take on the narrow mountain paths and the dirt road easily.

Federal Land Campgrounds

Federal campgrounds include lands managed by the United States Forest Service (USFS), Army Corps of Engineers (COE), and the Bureau of Land Management (BLM).

The National Parks are also included in this list. You will find that campgrounds located in the National Parks are going to be a bit more expensive. Because of this, you can find more amenities in the more popular National Parks like Yellowstone - which has shower and laundry facilities - and the Grand Canyon, which has convenience stores. National Parks are also very popular, and it is not uncommon to find them fully booked for months in advance. So you should take note that the reservations open up 6 months prior while some open their reservation in windows.

Campgrounds under the COE or Army Corps of Engineers are usually on the bigger side and with partial hookups. However, the campgrounds in the USFS and BLM lean more on the primitive side. So do not expect access to fresh water or electricity - a few picnic tables and some fire rings are sometimes all you will get.

You can camp in these grounds for 2 weeks to a month, and most will open in seasons, so check carefully before you plan your trip. Reservations can be made in recreation.gov, but it is also good to talk to the park rangers and ask for their advice on where you can camp for free. More often than not, they will be happy to help you and point you to an amazing campground that won't cost a thing.

Another one managed by the federal government is the National Wilderness Areas. These are often parts of the National Parks and Forests themselves as well as wildlife refuges. These make up for 4.8 percent of the total landmass of the country, and most allow regulated hunting. During the peak seasons, most of the campsites under the National Wilderness Areas would need you to obtain permits in case you want to hike or camp, but it is free during the off-season. This is done to help manage the traffic of incoming people to help protect the land, the animals, the trees, and the forest.

State Park Campgrounds

State park campgrounds are owned by, as you may have guessed, the State. Because of this, the state of the campground will vary wildly from State to State. States that have more funding will, of course, have better-managed parks, but almost all will have partial hookups and even a common dump station for RV sewage. Some amenities will also be provided in the form of bathrooms, shower stalls, and laundry facilities. Most will also offer recreational sports for you to participate in. The main difference I have found between these State Parks and the National Parks is that the State parks tend to be a lot bigger than their federal counterpart. The grounds are bigger - even the road is bigger.

County Park Campgrounds

Perfect for families with kids, the county parks are

located nearest to the cities. They're perfect for beginners too. Some of the parks offer partial hookups and a few simple amenities like showers and laundry.

RV Parks - $35 to $50 Per Night

(May Provide Partial Hookups to Full)

These campgrounds are scattered all across the country in varying sizes and amenities. Some are small, while others pretty much function as a chain of campgrounds that have different locations across the country. Amenities will also vary. Some can provide almost everything you need, from full hookups to a clubhouse, free Wi-Fi, and cable TVs to sites that look more or less like the government-owned campgrounds, surrounded by trees and partial hookups.

Prices will vary greatly depending on the location, amenities, size, and age of the campsites. Older parks are smaller, cheaper, and will offer fewer amenities. But most will offer some kind of membership. This is especially useful if you plan to go camping a handful of times a year. Some campgrounds are members of some kind of membership program that can offer you discounted bookings, like Passport America. Chain campsites also have their own membership programs.

RV Resorts - $50 and Above

(Provides Full Hookups)

The RV resorts are going to be the A-list celebrities in this group. These campgrounds or resorts, as they're more aptly called, will provide you with everything you can think of, from full hookups to water slides, Jacuzzis, and spas.

Chapter 6: On Meals and Menus: Simple Recipes

You will want to approach car camping with a sense of fun and adventure. If you are going to do car camping for the first time, it is understandable that you will feel nervous about a lot of things. For me, I was most worried about cooking outside. I was never a good girl scout when I was younger, but necessity and stress for me are always good teachers. I also hate washing dishes, so I try to cook everything in one pot and also eat in that same pot - except, of course if I'm going to take pictures of it for the 'gram.

Come to think of it, that laziness might have helped me perfect the art of cooking in one propane stove or grill. You see, the first thing you need to understand is that when cooking in the great outdoors, you won't have access to a lot of things you are used to in a regular kitchen at home. You won't have huge counter space. You will probably only be able to use one propane stove, and therefore only one pot or pan can be used at any given time. You will not have a sink beside you, and you'll only have access to limited condiments and spices. If you are the type of cook who fancies laying out all of the ingredients in front of you like you're in a cooking show, then you'll probably struggle with cutting down on your steps.

The key here is to minimize the steps, the ingredients, and of course, the washing up. Depending on your location, you might not have access to water - fresh or not - for washing up.

Cooking in the Wild

So, here are a few reminders on how you can properly cook in the wild without losing your mind:

Plan your meals ahead of time.

Although spontaneity is fun, planning your meals ahead of time will help you out greatly if you are new to this. This way, you can plan and pack all the necessary ingredients all properly portioned out for your trip - it will be easier to just throw them all in one pot when you arrive at your destination. By doing this, you can save a lot of storage space in your car by only packing everything that you will need.

Prep your ingredients the day before.

Of course, you could also or buy the ingredients on your way to the camp.

As I said, counter space will be lacking most of the time, especially if you are boondocking. Unless you know that you are going to camp in a place where there are picnic tables, then it would be faster for you to actually cut and slice all your ingredients and place them in separate bags for ease of use.

Another way of approaching this is when you are already familiar with the place you are going to go to. You can stop by the nearest store on your way to the camp to buy your ingredients. You will probably save more money, though, if you prepare things beforehand, but buying the ingredients on the way to camp can ensure that everything is fresh.

Pack small.

If you like to buy your condiments in large bottles and bags, decant them and store them in mini containers. You do not need to pack 3 gallons of cooking oil in your car.

Reduce your cooking steps.

One-pot cooking is your best friend. This trend has been gaining traction since before the pandemic, and it continues to this day. There are now dedicated cookbooks for one-pot or one-pan meals. It's lazy cooking, glamorized, as some would say, but for me, it is a form of efficient cooking. It will also taste the same anyway - most of the time. Let me also add to this that you may want to explore aluminum foil cooking too.

Learn to love your propane stove.

You don't actually need a campfire in order to cook things while you are camping. You might have had to before in the '50s, but the years have been kind, and now we have a lot of things we can use instead of a roaring campfire that can be quite hard to maintain. You can, for instance, use self-heating meal boxes that you can just buy online and an electric kettle. Yes, you can bring an electric kettle when you are camping, but my favorite thing to use is my portable propane stove. First, there's no smoke. Second, I can control the fire, so my eggs aren't overdone. Third, I don't have to gather wood at night just to feed the fire. Frankly, the list goes on, but I'm going to stop right here.

Of course, I'll also let you in on a few ultra-simple recipes that lazy ol' me loves to prep in a jiffy when enjoying the great outdoors. Without further ado, I present to you my beloved camping recipes. These are also great options when you're tired from a long and hard day at work and choosing food from Uber Eats takes around 2 hours.

Breakfast Recipes

Easy Scrambled Eggs

Everyone knows how to make scrambled eggs, but

adding mayonnaise makes it creamy without adding milk - which can go bad quickly. I buy the ones sold in the Asian stores that are packed in small squeeze bottles.

1 egg

1 teaspoon of water

2 teaspoons of mayonnaise

Salt and pepper

Oil or butter

Crack the egg in a bowl and mix in all the ingredients together until well blended. Place the pan over the fire and heat your oil. When the oil is hot, pour the egg mixture into the pan and whisk with a fork briskly until the eggs start clumping up. Take off the heat and eat with a slice of white bread.

Spam and Egg Sandwich

1 egg

1 thick slice of spam

Salt and pepper

Bread

Place the skillet over the fire and heat a small amount of oil. Fry up the sliced spam. When one side is crispy to your liking, flip it and add the egg in. Cook the egg the way you like it. Eat with a piece of bread.

Campfire Hash

1 large potato, diced

2 to 3 cloves of garlic, diced

Half a large onion, diced

Bacon or diced pieces of ham or spam

4 eggs, scrambled

2 tablespoons of mayonnaise

Salt and pepper

Cooking oil or butter

Heat a pan or a wide-bottomed pot. Heat oil and sauté diced garlic and onion in a skillet. Add in the diced potatoes and fry until crispy, and the potatoes can be easily mashed with just your fingers. Add in the scrambled eggs, mayonnaise, butter, salt, and pepper. Mix well until combined. You can also top it with some grated or sliced cheese.

Lunch Recipes

Quick Soup Pasta

Half a cup of dried macaroni

1 large tomato, cut roughly

1 clove of garlic, diced

¼ onion, diced

2 slices of bacon or spam

Salt and pepper

1 egg, scrambled

1 cup of water

Heat a pot and add some oil. Quickly sauté the diced garlic and onions, then add in the tomatoes. When the tomatoes start to become mushy, add the slices of bacon and quickly fry them to bring out the pork fat. Add water and then the macaroni. Cover the pot and let it sit for a few minutes in the fire to let it boil. When the macaroni is cooked, slowly pour in the egg while stirring slowly. Season with a bit of salt and pepper to taste, then serve.

Buttered Chicken Steak

1 piece of chicken steak

Butter

3 cloves of garlic, diced

In a hot pan, add oil and sauté the diced garlic until crispy. Set this aside, then add in the chicken steak with the skin side facing down. Fry it in the garlic oil until the skin is crispy before flipping it. Add a teaspoon of water into the pan and let the chicken cook covered. When both sides are cooked, flip it once again, so the skin side is facing down again to crisp it up. Serve with a side of vampire hash or mashed potatoes. Top with the crispy garlic.

Cheesy Steak in a Wrap

¼ pound of tenderloin beef, diced

2 cloves of garlic, diced

¼ onion, diced

Lots of cheese

In a hot pan, add oil and sauté the diced garlic and onion until fragrant. Add in the diced beef and toss until the surface is lightly charred, but the insides are still juicy. Toast your wrap. You can use a pita wrap or even a soft tortilla; taco shells also work. Place the beef on a row of fresh diced tomatoes and top with loads of cheese. Close the wrap and serve.

Vegetables in Foil

1 cup of mixed vegetables, carrots, string beans, cucumber, etc.

Salt and pepper

butter

Place the diced mixed vegetables in foil wrap. Season it generously with salt and pepper, then add a dab of butter on top. Close the wrap and place this atop a grill and cook for 5 minutes. After 5 minutes, open the top slightly and let the steam come out. Let it cook for another 1 minute. Poke the vegetables with a fork to check if they are done cooking. Serve.

Dinner Recipes

Beef in a Foil

¼ pound of tenderloin beef, diced

2 cloves of garlic, diced

1 large potato, diced

Salt and pepper

In a piece of foil, place a bed of potatoes on it and top it with the diced beef. Drizzle olive oil on it and season with salt and pepper. Close the foil up and place it on top of a grill. Leave it cooking for 5 minutes before checking to see if the beef is done to your liking. If it is, leave the foil open for 1 minute or so before serving.

Quick Pork and Mushroom Sauté

¼ pound of sliced pork

2 cloves of garlic, diced

¼ onion, diced

Half a cup of mushrooms

Half a cup of carrots or any vegetable you have on hand

Salt and pepper

Soy sauce

In a piece of foil, layer the vegetables, the mushrooms and the sliced pork on top of the other. Season every layer with a dash of salt and pepper, then add in the diced garlic and onions. Before closing the wrap, add in a dash of soy sauce for flavor. Close the wrap and place the foil wrap on top of the grill and let it cook for 5 to 8 minutes. After 5 minutes, check the meat and the vegetables if it's done - continue cooking if not. When done, open the foil pack and let it rest for a minute before serving.

A Word On Campfires and Bears

Camping, for some, might be synonymous with campfires. There's always that image of leisurely cooking over campfires, singing a song or two, and telling ghost stories that you'll regret later on in the night. But to tell you the truth, I think campfires only add to the aesthetic of camping most of the time (Gasp! Don't crucify me).

You should know that campfires are a hassle to start, and you will probably have to bring your own firewood too. Shocking, I know, but the cardinal rule in camping is that you can only collect deadwood on the forest floor. You cannot and should not cut off branches from living trees. If a ranger sees you, you will have to pay a fine. Also, it is not good for the environment - the trees need the nutrients they get from the rotting food on the forest floor. It's an ecosystem, and you are just a visitor - usually an unwanted one.

But first things first - there are a few rules you need to know before you embark on starting a campfire yourself.

Here, I am going to assume that you will be boondocking somewhere like the grounds under BLM. As I said above, you are going to be a visitor, and you must respect the place and the people that might be there camping too. Do not disturb the place and make your mark there. We, humans, have already destroyed so much - don't destroy what is left of nature too. The keyword here is to leave everything the way you found it. It may sound too much, but we need to be responsible for all our actions - and campfires are one tradition that might be causing a lot more harm than you think.

Building a Fire

Before you build a fire, you must be responsible enough to ask yourself a couple of these questions:

Will starting a fire here destroy or harm the environment?

What is the season? Do you really need to start one for cooking or heat if you have a portable stove anyway?

Are there existing restrictions in place where you want to set up camp?

Is there an appropriate place for you to start a fire?

Is there enough deadwood found on the forest floor? You don't want to gather all the deadwood - those provide nutrients for the trees and habitat for various woodland creatures.

That said, here are a few things to remember when looking to build a campfire:

Look for existing fire rings. Don't just throw wood anywhere you want to and start a fire. If there's none, think twice before you start one. More often than not, you will need to apply for the necessary permits in order to build your own campfire, so always ask permission first.

Bring your own firewood.

Choose locations that are away from any vegetation, shrubs, or trees. Do not place the fire next to a tree and under the canopy. The smoke will destroy the tree and endanger any animal living upon the branches.

Keep 100 feet away from any water source. The vegetation growing near water is much more delicate.

Keep away from meadows and clearings.

If you are to build a campfire, follow these steps:

1. To build a fire ring where there is none.

Choose your site. Do not build a fire on healthy soil - it will sterilize it, and we don't want that. The bed of a fire ring should be made of gravel or mineral soil. Surround it with a rock ring.

2. Firewood.

You will need tinder, kindling, and firewood. Tinder is small twigs and dry leaves that can burn easily and quickly. Kindling is made of small sticks about an inch in width, while firewood will make your fire last longer through the night. Do not bring firewood from home. Campgrounds and stores that allow campfires will gladly sell you bundles of kindling and firewood. Bringing firewood from home adds the risk of introducing insects that are not native to the forest. Never cut branches off trees in the forest.

3. Building and lighting the campfire.

There are three ways on how you can build a campfire: the cone, log cabin, and the pyramid.

For the cone, start with a small pile of kindling and tinder at the center of your fire ring. Once the fire gets going, add a few larger logs, a few at a time.

In the log cabin method, place two pieces of firewood in the middle with a bit of room in between. Stack two smaller pieces on top of the first layer to form a square. Place tinder and kindling in the middle and cover it with more firewood. These should get smaller and smaller as you go up. Top it with a layer of tinder and kindling, then light your fire. Make sure there are enough gaps between the logs to let the oxygen flow through.

When making the pyramid, you start by arranging 4 of your biggest logs side by side at the bottom of your fire ring. On top of this, add smaller logs in a perpendicular direction. The shape should get smaller as you reach the top. Place the tinder and kindling on the top and light your fire.

4. How to extinguish and clean up your campfire.

Extinguish the fire by pouring water over it, not sand or soil. These will not completely kill the fire like water would. Check the ashes before leaving your site. It should be cool to the touch, and when you bury your hand in the ash, you should not get burned. Scatter the ash over a broad area, and if you have pieces of charcoal, crush it and scatter them too.

Dealing with Bears

Now, one of the main dangers a camper might come face-to-face with is a bear. Here's the thing: bears do not hunt humans. If you do come across a bear when you are camping, it is not looking for you - it is looking for food. Bears are also not aggressive, and they will generally avoid people too. They are also curious creatures, so if you see a bear standing up on its hind legs, it's not aggressive - it only wants to get a better look at things. They are not territorial.

Other things you should take note of are the types of bears you can encounter in the wild. There are three: the grizzly bears or the brown bears, the black bears, and the polar bears. Since the black bears and the brown bears are the most commonly encountered during camping, I am only going to discuss the two.

The grizzly bears are the most dangerous land mammal that can be found in North America. The Alaskan brown bear and the grizzly bear are the two subspecies, with the Alaskan brown bear being the larger. They are around four and a half feet from shoulder height when they are standing on all fours. The grizzly bear is smaller than the Alaskan brown bear by a full feet. Their habitat is in the northwestern parts of the United States, Alaska, and Canada. They usually won't climb trees, but they will if they want to.

The black bears are the most common bears in the United States and can be found in all 50 states. They are the smallest of the 3 bear species that can be found in the United States. They are mostly gentle, shy, and evasive with furs that range from black, brown, to blond. They can also climb trees very well and can be usually seen hanging about in the higher branches.

With that out of the way, here are a few pointers on how you can prevent a bear from wandering into your camp.

1. Bring bear spray.

Pack bear spray with you on all your camping trips. If you are camping in bear country, a bear spray may save your life.

2. Do not be too quiet.

I know peace and solitude is what you like when you go boondocking, but making some noise, especially if you are alone in bear country, will alert the bear of your presence, and they will mostly avoid you. This is a crucial step to avoid a tense confrontation with a bear. So play some music, sing or talk, and bang some pots and pans if you like.

3. Avoid going solo.

Even though car camping is a fun activity when you are by yourself, do not plan to go into bear country. If you are, plan on bringing a friend with you.

4. Choose your campsites well.

Survey the ground well before you pitch your tent or pull out the camping gears. Look for any signs that a bear might have been there, like scratched trees, discarded food, bear prints, and poop.

5. Do not bring your dog.

A dog is very protective of its owner. If you bring a dog into bear country and it meets a bear, it might show aggression towards the bear when it's protecting you, and it might start growling and barking. This may provoke and make the bear attack.

6. Don't go near a bear.

Not even for Instagram likes. Even getting close to the bear cubs can get you killed.

7. Keep a can of bear spray and flashlight when you sleep.

Bears have good night vision, so sleep with a headlamp on you or next to you. Also, hold on to a can of bear spray.

8. Keep the food smells away.

Keeping the food smells away from your camp is a good practice that can keep the bears away from your camp. A tactic you can use is what campers usually call the "bear-muda." Form a triangle with your sleeping quarters (tent or car), your food storage, and on the last corner, the campfire where you cook your food. Even the dripping in the fire may attract animals. Place your tent upwind from your food, then pack everything in airtight containers before storing them in your car with all the windows rolled up. As an extra precaution, you can also choose to change into clean clothes after cooking and eating.

9. Keep clean.

Wash everything after you have cooked and eaten a meal. Do not just leave them out with crumbs. That can also attract bears.

And if you do meet a bear, make a lot of noise and try to make yourself as large as possible. Don't turn around and run. Face the bear and slowly back away. If it still approaches you, use the bear spray.

In the worst-case scenario where the bear attacks, different bears require different approaches. If it's a brown bear, play dead. Grizzlies can be aggressive and attack when they want to protect their cubs. So lie flat on the ground, face down with your legs and elbows spread. Cover the back of your neck with your hands. If the bear rolls you over, roll over once more so you are still facing the ground. By doing this, you are showing the grizzly that you are not a threat, and they might leave you alone if it's a defensive attack.

Black bears, on the other hand, are shy by nature and would not attack. But during the times that they do, the attacks are going to be predatory. So you will need to fight back really hard. Usually, when the black bear notices that there is resistance, it will back off.

Chapter 7: Survival 101

I mentioned I wasn't a girl scout back then, but I did still pick up a thing or two during my car camping days. While I'm no Bear Grylls, I know how to purify water, at the very least, which is an essential skill when push comes to shove and you've run out of drinking water.

Water

To make sure that the water you drink doesn't have any kind of bacteria, you can always simply use a kettle over a campfire to boil it. It should take you about 4 to 5 minutes to boil 1 liter. Just be sure that you place a grill plate over your campfire ring to keep your kettle stable - you wouldn't want it to spill over, or worse, burn you.

If, of course, you're at a campsite with an electrical outlet, by all means, use an electric kettle. You can also invest in an internal flame kettle or a Ghillie Kettle, which can easily boil water in just 2 minutes. As the name suggests, you can light a fire inside the kettle itself to heat up your water. You can also power your kettle from your car's cigarette lighter if you have an adaptor for it (just be wary of draining your car's battery). For a real emergency, you can use a tin can to boil water, but do be wary of handling the hot can (as well as the bacteria in the can itself). You can put the can in the fire first to kill off the bacteria before attempting to boil water in it.

Aside from boiling, you can use filters and chemical tablets. I'll talk about the former in a bit, but for the latter, good brands such as Potable Aqua can help purify your water by using chemicals (such as iodine) to kill off any nasty bacteria. They might alter the taste of the water, though, and may not be too effective against some protozoa.

As for portable water filters, they help strain out microscopic nasties and are compact and lightweight to boot. Try to aim for a filter efficiency of fewer than 0.4 microns. You might want to combine chemical tablets and water filters but do be sure you don't have an iodine allergy, thyroid disease, or other immunodeficiencies. Also, be wary of your filter clogging. If your filters use carbon, check the manufacturer's recommendations as to when you should replace the filters and the carbon element.

Shelter

As for other survival measures, you can learn how to make an emergency shelter (you never really know when you might need one) when sudden storms strike or whatnot. For instance, you can try to use a tarp or plastic shelter to form a lean-to or wedge tent. You can even use pegs, stones, or sticks to secure the edges.

Food

When it comes to food, you may be able to get by with wild fruits and plants, but remember only to gather them where it's legal. Don't remove plants if it might erode the soil, and collect only what you will be using. It's very dangerous to haphazardly ingest random plants, so some knowledge of toxins is always handy. Don't eat the ones near well-traveled roads as these may contain high lead levels. If you see any other creatures snacking at the pants, then they're likely edible, but always double-check. Most of the time, plants with milky sap or juices and those with blackened leaves are a big no-no.

Getting Help/Getting Lost

Just in case something untoward happens to you, signaling for help in an emergency situation may mean the difference between life and death. You can find an open area and prep 3 fires that are arranged in a triangle. If you can't make each side measure about 3 meters, try to make 3 fires in a row instead. Once the fire is lit, be sure to keep a safe distance. The fire should be able to catch the attention of others in the vicinity, so only do so if you think there are others in the area.

If you ever get lost, you can try to find North by looking at the stars. If you see the Big Dipper, the two stars at the end of it should point to a brighter, more fixed star. This is the North Star or Polaris, so facing this star means you are facing north.

Keep Healthy

Obviously, survival also means keeping healthy even when you're on the road, and no, it's not just about eating a well-balanced diet. Don't go the lazy "fast food" route all the time, not if you don't want to shorten your life span.

When you can, try to get moving - just the simple act of taking a walk by the nearby trail can already work wonders on your health. You'll feel better, and you'll get to spend some time with nature too - or better yet, go for a quick swim if you're near a body of water. Try to incorporate any kind of movement into your daily routine to keep yourself healthy and fit.

Chapter 8: Making A Living While Camping

A few years before, I stopped doing remote work in favor of actually going back to the office. Shocking, I know, but I missed being with the people in the office and actually talking to people. I had been remote working for a few years after I started to live in my car. I love the outdoors so much that I picked up remote working after numerous stressful office jobs. After I walked out of my last office job, I thought, "This is freedom - I'm never going back again."

So I went out, bought an SUV, and started traveling. I had enough funds saved up - I was planning to use it for a mortgage - but I wanted to do something crazy at the time, so I started plotting my course and off I went. All this was years ago. I went back to my drab office life. Had fun hanging out with my old friends for a while, then the pandemic happened. I got stuck working from home, all alone in my apartment, itching to go out. So when the lockdowns lifted, I got my old gear out and hit the road again.

Remote working is thriving, and I find that it is so much easier now to do it. Because of the pandemic, companies now are realizing that "Hey! Maybe we don't need to have all the employees in one building. We can cut back on overhead costs too!" Also, when most of us are working from home, it's easy to just work anywhere we want to - as long as you're responsible and do your jobs on time, that is.

Utility Considerations

Internet Connection

The most important thing when it comes to working

remotely is your internet connection. I have a wireless hotspot and my mobile data from my phone - that's nearly 50 GB of data per month. It's not enough for me most of the time since I watch a lot of movies and TV series in my spare time, but the data is unlimited, and when the 50 GB cuts out, I'll still have internet, but the speeds slow down drastically especially during peak hours.

But since I live in my car, it's kind of hard to properly work without tables. I mean, sure, I can work sprawled on my bed in my tent. But that would just make my back hurt like hell. But lucky for us, co-working spaces are popping up all over the country, and I can just pop in quickly for a few days a week to finish my tasks. If I'm going to be in that city for an extended period of time, I also usually rent a private office in the space so I can leave my work things locked safely in there. But if there are no co-working spaces nearby, there's still bound to be a Starbucks around the corner. For the price of a coffee, I would shamelessly stay half a day just to use their free Wi-Fi.

Mail and Deliveries

My mail and deliveries are much harder. Some more

established campsites will accept and hold your mail and deliveries, but then you do need to schedule and time your trips. Another option that is available to you is to get your mail delivered to the post office, but you will need to call ahead and confirm because not all post offices can accept mail and deliveries. Though recently, I've moved all my correspondence and bills to my email, and if there's mail to be received, I just forward all of them to my sister's house up in Maine. For deliveries, I choose to pick up my items myself in Amazon Hub lockers and Counters.

Electricity and Power

Another thing you will need is, of course, electricity and power. Car camping doesn't mean you have to be totally cut off from the civilized world. If you are remote working, you will need your chargers, so bring with you some of the generators in case you go boondocking, and there are no hookups available. It is also a good idea to add solar panels as a backup.

Change Your Tires

Fully kitted-out SUVs are expensive. To enjoy your time outdoors, all you need is a 4 wheel drive and good tires. Both of these are enough to get you to where you want to go without spending a pretty penny.

Modifications

You won't need a permanent bed at the back of your car if you are just going car camping on the weekend. However, if you are going to be sleeping in your car for an extended trip, it might be more reasonable to do modifications to your car.

Not all modifications are supposed to be permanent. You can just remove the seats from the back and add in a modified single-sized bed inside instead. By doing so, you won't need to fold down the seats every night and prepare your bed. You will also free up a lot of storage space underneath the bed if you built it with a bed frame on legs. Adding straps and organizers can secure various storage boxes against the wall if you are traveling.

For people planning to live in their cars for a year or so, more modifications can be done to make your time more comfortable, even under budget. You can build and fit in cabinets and cubby holes as well as a folding bed. And if you think there's not enough rear storage space in your vehicle, I've seen jaw-dropping hatchback conversions while I'm on the road. It just takes a bit of planning. And if you are good with your hands, you can probably build the modifications yourself.

Chapter 9: Camp Etiquette and Safety

I think I said it before: camping is a privilege, not a right. Even if your goal is boondocking, there will be times when you will find yourself among other humans, especially if you are going to need hookups.

Etiquette

But neighbors or no neighbors, there are a few camping rules that you will need to follow:

Respect your neighbor's space because not all campsites will have you hundreds of feet apart from your next human neighbor. Also, don't just walk through your neighbors' space to get anywhere. Use the camp-provided footpaths.

Greet your neighbors. A simple good morning when you see them outside will do. This is a great way to remove the awkwardness whenever you see them, and also, people tend to be nicer if you are on speaking terms with them.

Cut back on noise. If you are in bear country all alone for hundreds of miles, then yes, make some noise. But if you are in a designated campground, chances are there will probably be neighbors. Keep the music and the laughter down, especially at night.

Corral your children and pets, so they stay inside your designated campground space, however cute you think they are - besides, not everyone will think the same way. Do not let them run around in reckless abandon.

Leave everything as you found them. When you leave, take with you everything you have set out, even the trash. It should look like nobody was there. This is especially true when you are boondocking.

Respect nature. Don't disturb the trees, plants, animals, etc. You are there to enjoy their company and observe, not disturb. If you see a squirrel, don't run around to catch it just to take a nice picture for the 'gram or TikTok. Leave it alone.

If you find yourself near a water source, camp at least a hundred feet away from it. Not only will you be keeping yourself safe from unexpected flash floods, but you will also be doing the ecosystem near the water a favor. These plants near water are a lot more delicate, so camp away from them. You can get water from them if they are safe to drink, but never pee, defecate or wash your clothes or your pots and pans in there.

Camp in already disturbed or impacted surfaces. It might look good to camp in the middle of a meadow or a field of flowers, but please don't. A single night of sleeping on top of them will no doubt kill them. So If there is a bare spot of earth or soil that looks like people had been camping there, use that space instead.

Do not modify the surroundings just to set up your camp. If you find a good view but the ground is not level, or there are plants and shrubs in the middle, do not cut them down. Just move on and look for a more suitable campsite. Moving and cutting things in the forest is not something you should do just for a few nights' stay. These have their own ecosystems, so try not to disturb them.

Going to the toilet is not hard if you don't have an RV. All you need is a trowel and a hole. If you are going to pee and poop in the wild, dig a hole at least two hundred feet from any water source - around 70 steps. Dig a hole 6 inches deep. Do your thing and cover it back up. If you are using the normal bathroom and toilet paper, do not bury it with your excrement. It doesn't decay. Use a leaf - as long as it's not poisonous - or a squirt bottle filled with water as a portable bidet.

If you bring a dog, pick up after your dog. If it poops, pick it up and bring it out with you. Also, don't let it catch and play with the smaller wildlife.

Do not feed the animals. What we eat and what they eat are different. By feeding them our human food, we will be doing more harm than good.

Safety

When it comes to safety, remember that you should not be taking it for granted. When out camping, you are in danger of getting attacked not only by wildlife but also by humans. According to some campers, the only thing scarier than bears is a crazy human, especially if they have a gun. So it pays to take a good look at your surroundings before you set up camp.

If you are sleeping in your car, you need to take some precautions too. There are going to be bad and desperate people willing to take advantage of you if you are too trusting or too nice. It might even turn you into a target, especially if you are out there all alone. Here are a few things you should keep in mind if you plan to do car camping:

Close all doors and the windows when you sleep, not even to let the fresh air in. This is especially true if you are in an urban setting, but it also applies when you are in a campsite. Someone could get in your car using that gap.

Do not leave the engine running when you are sleeping

inside. Carbon monoxide poisoning can lead to deaths. The fumes from your engine can seep into your car and cause oxygen deprivation.

Check your surroundings for red flags. Look for signs of drug use or if there are drunk and homeless people walking around. Trust your gut instinct. If something makes you feel uneasy, like unexpected sounds, broken glass, or a person staring at you, it is better to pack up and move.

Get proper rest. Don't drive at night. Accidents are more likely to happen if you are tired and are driving at night. Drive only if you are well-rested.

Don't pull over and park by the side of the highway. It is highly dangerous and also, a lot of times, illegal.

Be constantly aware of your surroundings, especially if you are among other people. Try not to get out of your car when you are already parked to go to sleep. There's a reason why you see van life and car camping YouTubers shimmying to the backseat from the front like fish when they are about to sleep. There's no need for the world to see that you are sleeping in the backseats of your car.

Use a blackout curtain to hide and separate the rear of your car from the front. Also, cover all your windows at night, even if you are just resting at the back. Don't let others see in and get any ideas.

Always park your car with the front facing the quickest escape. When things go wrong, it can go wrong quickly - so you should be prepared to escape quickly too. Keep your car keys, defense spray or bear spray, flashlight, and other defensive weapons close to you when you sleep. If you are stealth camping in random parking lots, don't leave things set up outside your car. If you hear things outside your car in the middle of the night, set off your car alarm to deter would-be thieves.

Purchase roadside assistance to get you out of trouble. Having a membership with AAA can give you a sense of peace. This is really important if you want to spend your days boondocking.

Know a bit about your car. Even though you have roadside assistance, it pays to know a bit about troubleshooting your car. Keep the car manual in your glove compartment. This is going to be your bible. If you are going to be driving for extended periods of time, you must know at least some of the basics, like changing a flat tire, jumping the battery, and checking the tire pressure and your oil.

Maintain your car well. Don't abuse it, especially if you are planning to be on the road for longer. I know someone who treated his Toyota Innova like a 4x4 and ended up getting stuck and towed. When you are in a city or town, get your car checked and serviced.

Aside from filling up the gas tank of your vehicle frequently, bring along an extra jug of fuel if you are going on long trips in the backcountry. Install the app "gas buddy" on your phone to help you pinpoint the nearest gas station.

Emergency Preparedness

Aside from the "10 essentials" for your survival, you must also keep these things inside your car in case of emergencies:

Jumper cables: Even if you are not going camping, you should have a jumper cable in your trunk as a precaution and know how to use it, of course.

A collapsible shovel: For the times your car gets stuck in the mud, dirt roads, and snow.

Portable air compressors: For your flat tires

Road flares: This makes you visible to other drivers in case you are met with a car emergency.

Consider adding security systems in your car if you are going to be living in it. Get wheel locks, hasp locks, steering wheel locks, pedal locks, and maybe even removable window bars. Motion sensor security lights and or alarms are even encouraged. Inconspicuous CCTVs mounted to the outside of your car can also be used to monitor the outside area when you are inside the vehicle. Add stickers that announce that you have a wild dog or even a GPS tracking alarm, even if you don't.

Add a compact safe in your car to store your laptop, gadgets, money, passports, and jewelry when you go hiking and bolt it to the chassis of your van.

Bring a flare, signaling mirrors and whistles with you. Signaling mirrors can be used to flash sunlight on incoming rescue planes or helicopters in case of emergency. Flares do the same as well as whistles.

Survival whistles can produce a high-pitched sound that can be heard across great distances.

Get a GPS vehicle tracking device in case someone does run off with your vehicle. It works like "where's my phone?" in your iPhone so you can track where your vehicle has gone to.

Camp in higher ground and away from bodies of water for ecological reasons and your own safety. Also, take note of the names of the bodies of water near your camp and check warnings of flash floods and dam openings before you hunker down for the night.

Don't pick up random hitchhikers regardless of gender. Sure, camping people generally are nice folks - they're chill and laid back, but there are a few bad apples out there.

Conclusion

When I made the decision to move into my car, my dad understood my life choices immediately - but it took a couple of years before I was able to tell my mom that I was actually living in my car. I knew my mother's fears were not unfounded; aside from the obvious security reasons, it was difficult to camp in a car, much less live in it. But if other people can live in it, why not me?

But even with all that posturing, I was basically, by all terms and definitions, homeless. The world wasn't as convenient as it is now, but my fabulous and tough-asnails '90s version couldn't care less.

The older or more "traditional" people in my life would stare at me in horror whenever my unique living situation was brought up in conversation. I could literally hear their minds say, "Oh, you poor child." A single girl living in her car in the '90s is not exactly frowned upon, but you can probably get the sentiment. It wasn't encouraged nor trendy at the time - not like it is now. What they couldn't grasp was that this was a conscious decision on my part.

Now, I have a small piece of the city that I call home. A nice Victorian townhouse with bare red brick walls. But my years in my small hatchback - to an SUV in the later years - would always be a fond memory for me. In some ways, camping in my car had given me a taste of an altogether different kind of freedom. Untethered and floating, it is still a very calming experience for me.

This is why I still go on car camping trips, a lot more than my peers, I'd like to think.

I feel a certain thrill now when I see that the reputation of car camping itself has improved drastically - especially now during the pandemic. With most commercial flights grounded, those bitten by the travel bug had to quench their wanderlust in other ways. Countries and businesses started to offer staycations and urged people to love and live local - to explore one's own backyard.

The pandemic has shifted the way people live, and it has opened a whole new world for car camping. Now, when you scroll through YouTube, you can see people vlogging about their car camping trips with pride. Even the "car camping" tag on Instagram had a tremendous boost in its numbers recently. Because car camping feels more spontaneous and free, it has recently become a choice favored by the younger generations.

Now, with a lot less things to worry about, car camping is perfect for people who don't need much because it can be as simple as you need it to be - a sleeping bag or even just warm blankets would do.

And if the back seats of your car folds down flat, that would be so much better because when you reach your destination, you can just easily lay a sleeping bag or an inflatable bed on top of it. And if you don't want to bother with any beds, the backseats are perfectly comfortable too!

I'm not trying to alienate any people here because car camping isn't just for the no "bells and whistles" demographic. In fact, you can be as extra as you want! Go ahead and bring along all sorts of items or gadgets to make your car camping trip as luxurious or extra as you want it to be. You can have everything from string lights to impressive tents - you will find that most people will have no qualms about bringing their own tents or even their favorite things along for a more comfortable sleeping experience.

Basically, the level of convenience and luxury you can experience when going on car camping trips will definitely depend on how much you are willing to bring and spend on your camping gadgets.

For example, I've seen people bring collapsible firewood ovens/heaters with them on trips to warm, fluffy, and heated carpets for their winter car camping trips.

At the end of the day, car camping may or may not be everyone's cup of tea - but with all of the benefits and the life-changing perspectives it can offer you, I definitely think it's worth a try for anyone at least once in your life.

It won't cost an arm and a leg, and it's a great learning

experience.

Made in United States
Troutdale, OR
10/16/2023